GARDEN ON AN ALIEN STAR SYSTEM

poems by

Judith Cody

Finishing Line Press
Georgetown, Kentucky

GARDEN ON AN ALIEN STAR SYSTEM

Copyright © 2020 by Judith Cody
ISBN 978-1-64662-343-3 First Edition
All rights reserved under International and Pan-American Copyright Conventions. No part of this book may be reproduced in any manner whatsoever without written permission from the publisher, except in the case of brief quotations embodied in critical articles and reviews.

ACKNOWLEDGMENTS

First Banquet after the Great Winter Siege ~ *Lyrical Passion Poetry* E-zine
Hose. Ants. Plants. Expressway. ~ *Qwerty Journal*
Rose of Sorrows ~ *The Arabesque Review* and on-line at *Arabesques-Press.com; RiverSedge; Ginosk*; and Honorable Mention from the National League of American Pen Women, 2009
Silver Rose of the Sea ~ *The Arabesque Review*
Ode to a Fistful of Soil ~ *Confluence*
Ode to the Flowers of Today ~ *RiverSedge; The Griffin, Lutheran Digest, Westview;* won the Director's Shortlist, Robert Frost Foundation 2008
Silence. Struggle. Salvation. ~ *Phantasmagoria*
Planet Under the Deck ~ on-line *Central California Poetry Journal*

Publisher: Leah Huete de Maines
Editor: Christen Kincaid
Cover and Interior Photos: Judith Cody
Author Photo: Herve Attia, TerrfficShot Photography
Cover Design: Elizabeth Maines McCleavy

Order online: www.finishinglinepress.com
also available on amazon.com

Author inquiries and mail orders:
Finishing Line Press
P. O. Box 1626
Georgetown, Kentucky 40324
U. S. A.

Table of Contents

Agave Parnei Cactus, photo

Missing the Garden 1

Hose. Ants. Plants. Expressway. 2

Hunt for the Moon in the Roses in the Dawn 3

Under the Landscape 4

Ode to a Fistful of Soil 5

Rose of Sorrows 6

Dinosaur Demeanor by the Ounce 7

Planet Under the Deck 8

Ode to the Flowers of Today 9

Kitchen Lady 10

Mirage on a Glacier 11

Silver Rose of the Sea 12

Stars Caught in a Spider's Web, photo

Justice by Hoe 14

Paths Must Be Found That Beguile 15

Eden. Remembrance. 16

Garden on an Alien Star System 17

Silence. Struggle. Salvation. 18

Ode to Don Juan 19

Just a Few Dozen Please 20

First Banquet After the Great Winter Siege 21

The Bulbs Have Counted Their Days 22

A Question of Power 23

Sanctuary 24

Solar Eclipse Shadows Through a Branch, photo

For my beloved husband, David

MISSING THE GARDEN

Missing the garden
Too far away from this
1923 art nouveau hotel
Lodged deeply within
Rundown central Los Angeles.

My room butts up against
A many-windowed air shaft
In the way of millions of rooms
Wedged within big cities'
Sprawl everywhere.

Some primal search gene
Signals my need to heed
Whatever may need heeding
Outside this particular
Window in the moment of now.

Young couple at right angles
To my survey squeaks open their sash
Both lean, bent double, out,
Her yard long hair tumbles downward
(Nice demo of the gravity principle).

His rough-tender hand gesture
Pulls her hair back; her head arches,
Lips screwed, she spits a thick mix
(White contrast flows near brown brick)
Merrily watches it smack the bottom.

HOSE. ANTS. PLANTS. EXPRESSWAY.

It seems an odd thing to be concerned with three hundred or so linear feet of supple, green garden hose. Yes, but the hose is something much more than a transporter of water to the plant denizens of backyard. Beginning at the back wall of the old house, the green water pipeline's journey is a circuitous one as it curls across the gravely earth, arcing gracefully (not to put a kink in itself), among the shrubs, around the various trees, fruit and whatnot, lain carefully not to rub against smaller tender plants, finally all is in perfect alignment with principle, then may the copper knob—verdigris polished to a golden gleam by the gardener's grasp—be cautiously twisted to open the worn, leaky valve degree by degree until pressure is correct for proper water drinking by the herbage sprawling thirstily everywhere. But listen: even a grain of ground is a hill to an ant, and the soil is billions of torturous hill-climbs to reach an ant's countless microcosmic destinations throughout every day. All that was it; until the invention of the smooth hose expressway for ants; you see nowadays, steady ant traffic rolls quietly on its way, on the glorious Passageway of Hose. Scalding after-noontime-has-passed sun excites the tiny ant-mobiles into their mad rush hour commute to their domicile. But unlike others, they behave with their own little dashes of dignity. No grid lock. No road rage. *Serenity of Purpose, Adaptation Now,* proclaim their bumper stickers.

HUNT FOR THE MOON IN THE ROSES IN THE DAWN
For Jenny

Daybreak broke wide apart the perils of bleak-dark night, beginning something new and glorious with a generous offering of the full spectrum of sunlight diffusing varied angstroms of fresh, new colorations on and about the magnificent nubile buds of the Don Juan climber. Nothing like this had ever been noted before in precincts of the Rose garden. Strange-beauty of unbeknownst light on special roses demanded capture immediately; the call of command rose like a broken fire hydrant surging throughout the calm dawn time. Instant control of the rapidly fading dawn-light-situation must be commandeered by the dirt-digging, rose-planting, grime-knuckled gardener. She scurries indoors. Plucking the digital camera from its warm cradle, the photo-journalist-gardener hastily tried to recall all the quirks of this nouveau instrument of delight and anxiety. "Which tiny black button turns off the flash; turns on the camera; turns on the close-up lens; opens the shutter; does the shutter need opening; is there a shutter; where is the mode switch; what mode am I in anyway; what's a mode?" Bending in supplication before the fifteen foot tall, rusted trellis that allowed the juvenile Don Juan freedom to roam upward, the artist-eyed gardener closed in on the buds, peered between two of them as if through a telescope, and beheld the morning moon dangling like an opal between the lush, deep velvet red, tight blooms. Sweat gathered in an eyelash blurring the rare rose scene delicately as dew. Both buds with the moon caught between them must all be permanentized—somehow—in the next brief moments as moon moves very fast when setting low on the horizon, thinks the astronomer-gardener. Press down tiny black button. Photo? No. Press down slim silver button. Photo. Yes. But no moon. Where'd the moon go? Parallax! Shift position. Correction noted. Photo. Yes. No moon. Where is it? Whoops—moon is behind the rose. Poor correction. Dawn sun rises higher, quickly alters light circumstances on roses, drowns out pale, lovely moon. The camera is nestled carefully back into its warm cradle where it continues sucking current from the gardener's house. All is ordinary again in the small rose garden where now the birds twitter prosaically as usual, the Don Juan seems just an unexceptional gentleman, so the gardener kneels down and goes back to valiantly yanking out sprawling clumps of crabgrass that have invaded from some other yard to steal micronutrients from the great rose shrubs.

UNDER THE LANDSCAPE

Winter: quietude of growth,
Slumbering insects,
Then the very soil's
Hibernation, all shelter
From the cold shroud
Left by the sun's
Departure since time
Began.

Spring: whisper of warmth,
Sly caresses on dozing
Tap roots, bulbs,
Stirred sap wells upward,
Warm kisses urge
Juices to rise,
To arouse
Cambium stems,
Bud cells—
Emerge and triumph
Over ice.

ODE TO A FISTFUL OF SOIL
After Pablo Neruda

Applause to the dark loam
Whose gentle brown worms, desperate
For damp cover, struggle deeper
Into that which they will become.

Wonders of molecules,
Primal lives slide
Through fingers gripping
Clay, sand, water, humus, air,
Prevailing, prevailing.

Exaltations to dinosaur, microbe,
Macrobe, mammal, insect, spider, bug,
Bird, man, woman, both the nourished
And the nourishment, time-traveling
Through this third planet's regolith.[1]

Accolades to the worlds' rivers' alluvium soils,
To eons of winds' aeolian soils,
To tranquil residual soils,
To the ancient glacial travels of soils.

Honors to misunderstood mycorrhizae,
Massive underground veil of root-fungi
Merging with great roots of trees, roots of grasses,
Shrubs, and flowers where it provides, provides:
A fungal partner in provender.

Offerings of bouquets and garlands to Earth,
Receiving all that is and will be
Within her secluded innards of
Unsullied decay that is soil.

---

[1] The layers of Earth's soils in various states of chemical change, including topsoil together with the unconsolidated rock fragments residing on the deep bedrock are the regolith.

ROSE OF SORROWS

Her thin arm beckoned from a thread worn coat of no distinct colour, while the soft rain fell as a blessing over all, blurring the torn and whole together into a gentle bath of tender hues tinged with a sort of silveriness whenever the sun briefly glowed. Her blue-veined hand offered every passerby the stump of a garish pink bouquet of rose buds: "Please, please buy a rose!" she called against the damp breeze. Thus was the Rose of Sorrows bought then hurried home to a warm bright room; there under the brilliant bulb an unforgiving truth was exposed both bitter and harsh. On inspection, each pink bud revealed itself as not a bud at all, but merely an old, almost withered flower. Someone, the sad rose seller or perhaps a pandering lover, had carefully coiled a fine wire tightly around attempting to shape it into a new rose; to prevent the bruised petals from falling to their natural end on the earth. Each of the flowers tested not really pink but were a crispy-edged brown that had been dyed the gaudiest pink, not out of bad taste but merely to better conceal the death of petals. O yes, the heavy odour had been a deliberate squirt of fulsome drugstore concoction. Great history of beauty, romance, even the extended exacting arts of horticulturists brought down to this pathetic masquerade! Expectations of youth and beauty end with senility and dust. The wonder is: who has the deepest pain, the seller, the buyer, or the rose? Destinies intermingle for those who consort within the World of the Rose.

DINOSAUR DEMEANOR BY THE OUNCE

What was that sparkling blur
Speeding almost imperceptibly?
This minute humming bird
Two thimblefuls of flesh
Feathers, flights of fancy
Dashes into the stiff streams
Of an Ace's Hardware sprinkler
System, over and over again
He flirts in and out of the
Swift water spray until
This tiny descendent of dinosaurs
Finds a thin rose limb to
Lounge upon and there,
There he stays beneath the
Pelting drops and preens,
Fluffs, beats his wings,
Turns round and about
To fully douse the entirety
Of his awesome *hummingbirdness*.

PLANET UNDER THE DECK

Under the plank deck, slugs, snails
Living some sort of destiny
Not unlike our own it seems
Simple little travesty

On billions of humans evolved
Over struggling eons
Millions of mysteries dissolved
Within our moist neurons

Getting the great picture clear
Enough to find sustenance
For flesh but nothing to keep fear
Of dark, of death at abeyance.

ODE TO THE FLOWERS OF TODAY

Having no feet you race across
The garden to me on a breeze
Wafting your fresh bloomed perfume
You tempt me to rest beside your
New and brilliant beauty
Knowing that it will vanish
Too quickly
That my eyes
Will be the solitary
Observer of your
Magnificent performance
In the fleeting sunshine
I am compelled to
Remain beside you.

KITCHEN LADY

Deep within the kitchen garden where
Autumn's Lady of the Kitchen harvests
Her kitchen provender her kitchen-reddened
Hands seize *Allium cepa* by its mud-splattered
Green-tresses. Yank it out! Her favorite
Butcher knife frolics merrily, slippery in the
Kitchen lady's grip. Off with the Allium's head.
All's ready to scrub, to chop, to dice,
To heave into soup, whip into gravy, slice into stew,
Ladle inside mouths waiting like dozens of famished chicks
Screeching unrelentingly, "feed me, feed me!"
Kitchen-weary lady ponders a paradox of Amaryllidaceae,
The kinship of bulbous onion with Belladonna Lily
Paired side-by-side in her kitchen-door plot:
Ah, the one sharp-sweet; the other lovely-lethal.

MIRAGE ON A GLACIER
Winter solstice

Shortest day, as if the sun has
Been abducted
Longest night, as the trees snap
Beneath ice sheaths
Frozen air is dense
Suffused with
Scents of Arctic winds
In the sight of all that creates
Frozen environs for this yearly position
Far from the sun.

Only months ago the sun
Hugged our round blue world
Then, it seems, fields and gardens
Had erupted with a plentitude of blooms
Vegetative masterpieces
Cornucopias of incomparable fruits
Perfumeries of nasal delights
Palettes of living pastels and primaries
Bowers of bursting buds
Arches of swaying roses
Stands of exotic shrubs
Robust trees, the single
Ancient oak, the flamboyant
Japanese maple—
—can it have been?

SILVER ROSE OF THE SEA

Her hand brushed the waves
Parting them for the hundredth time
Searching for him,
For shadows of promise:
Grey turbulent sea
Revealed no image
Blank darkness reflected
Only her disconsolate self.

Decades later after the years
Ceased their fixed distress, she
Sought an answer from the sea
Seeking one last evening tide
To recall his face. Then she saw
Beneath moon-shimmered waves,
The Silver Rose, radiant,
But farther than the fullest
Breath of air might take her.

She knew at once
An answer to her primal grief.
Whispering waters enveloped
Her diving form, like an ancient
Embrace almost forgotten. Moonlight
Flickered on the surface of the sea
High above her head, swift
As an ocean being her arms arched,
Aimed her plunge down into deep
And darkening dreams where
She could reach the Silver Rose.

JUSTICE BY HOE
For Jeff

Shocking how suddenly they're there,
Rather appealing young weed sprouts
Carpeting all available ground
With a feathery amalgam of chartreuse
Where the yard reposed, bare as trout belly.

Knowing that in weeks these penny-sized
Delicate green leaves will burst into oversized
Brutes sucking nourishment from the roots of
Politically correct plants:
They must be sentenced, punished, destroyed.

PATHS MUST BE FOUND THAT BEGUILE

Away from kitchens
Away from porches
Away from windows
Away from doors
Away from inside anything.

Toward tools, rakes, hoes
Blades, shovels, silent ponds
Toward banks of waving flora
Toward under-canopies of trees
Toward horizons
Toward fresh drawn sun streams
Yellow as butter.

EDEN. REMEMBRANCE.
Would Proust remember?

A beam of sun finds a path onto the sill though the narrow opening at the top of this air shaft that corresponds in perimeter to the size of good garden almost anywhere in the world. But here on the pigeon feces crusted sill the sun will most likely stay but an hour or two with luck, at certain times of the year. When? What if I brought a small potted plant from the drugstore a block over; what if I allowed it residence here; would it be able to collect enough sun on its leaves so it could photosynthesize long enough to thrive? No, don't imagine it could survive. No. Not even a shadow garden. The real garden, as remembered, is already fading into a sort of personal myth of the garden. When people live this way—from the moment of birth onward—when human awareness is constantly burdened by massive shadows of steel, concrete structures; why then a lush, loamy place where there is the instinctual soothing presence of plants must surely take on a great legend status. Eden. That is, if you have never known such a space, is it possible to even envision the intense and personal green dimensions of an ordinary garden?

GARDEN ON AN ALIEN STAR SYSTEM

At 10 A.M. the window
Thermometer overlooking
The garden reads 90 degrees—
Heading toward a hundred degrees
Fahrenheit, and then some
As the day grows
Impatiently hotter
As if with hidden
Anger at the intolerable sun
Poking nosey flame-fingers
Into everything.

At 2 P.M. it is 103 degrees.
In semi-shade, the tender buds
Of multitudes of roses erupt
Into withered blooms, while
Swarms of geraniums rush
To flower and shrivel, then are
Burnt brown in hurried
Time lapse succession,
Their life cycle tremendously
Accelerated, concluded
Within a few hours.

At 4 P.M. it is 107 degrees. I swelter,
Fade, collapse, doing a fast forward
Morph into an ancient crone, like
The flowers speeding to their deaths
As if we are all circling
Some cruel star that is really
The imperious, living being
While all of us are merely
Its tiny toss-away toys.

SILENCE. STRUGGLE. SALVATION.
For Guy, he'd have understood

Crash in the rose garden. Crash. Crash. Crash.
Suddenly a full petaled wide open Tea Rose
Known as Mr. Lincoln, let go of most of
Its immense maroon, elderly petals (this all at once)
Sending them fluttering helplessly to the bare
Ground, some of them struck a furtive Brown Towhee
Who was scratching noisily at the base of the shrub
For a few errant earwigs who normally rest in the day,
But now must fight wiggle for their lives (though lost)
For a second, now the descending cascade of petals distracted
The disheveled bird allowing the exposed insects
To escape (this afternoon).

ODE TO DON JUAN
A rose who climbs balconies

Velvet darkest ruby cloak
Wraps Don Juan in the
Mystery of the Rose
Romeo-like he quickly climbs
His trellis to its
Highest point, there in
Lush profusion, his
Outrageous fragrance
Spills into all the
Secret arboretum places
Stroking long-forgotten
Fantasies, causing a curious
Light to infuse time.
No nook remains untouched.

JUST A FEW DOZEN PLEASE

All's well with armfuls of
Weighty long-legged roses.

Worldly things feel wonderful
When dozens of robust red roses

Are flung into my arms
Joining me by surprise

Like a celebrity boyfriend
Who is cooing, "You're beautiful. Uh huh!"

FIRST BANQUET AFTER THE GREAT WINTER SIEGE
For David

Where the roadway of
Constellations intersects
Sky's equator here
Is found the exact location
Of Spring (mislaid
For a year), Vernal
Equinox. Solar beams
Can wake the almost
Dead tree and flower roots
After their winter fast.

Frost still bites the
Air, yet it is now
When tender tips
Of newly sprouted
Leaves, and swelling buds
Aggressively jab
At air, hungrily stretch
To touch saffron rays of
Sun.

Photosynthesize!
Photosynthesize!
This command rises
From buried fresh
White root hairs
Springs to the
Apical meristem
At the very top of renewing
Apple, peach, pear trees,
All blossoming cousins in
The rose family, *Rosaceae*.
Now they must rush to eat
Their first dawn meal—
Our own close starlight
Washed down with
Last year's stockpiled sap.

THE BULBS HAVE COUNTED THEIR DAYS
To Chelsea

Memory is correct! Prompted
By the first clue to end-of-winter light
Green tips race upward from
Their buried bulbs
Certain of one existence strategy
Carefully honed over a
Few million years or so.

Today is their chosen moment
Their quintessence of allotted time
To twist emerald shoots toward the sky
As they risk or reach
Every atom of their potential
Then bask in that resplendent time.

A QUESTION OF POWER
Politics from the garden

A familiar aroma, but yet—
It causes us to notice
To forget our urgent chores
To turn and try to find
Where it's coming from.

The scent of a rose
Is something so known
So like other hypnotizing
Objects enticing us
To good or bad ends.

We know this much—
Lovers are lured to
Alter their lives by
This fragrance.

We know this much—
Perfume wafting
From an individual
Seemingly perfect rose has
Redirected history.

Trying to understand
This scent, can we see into
Ourselves
Then question
Other powers
We have allowed
To grow among us?

SANCTUARY
Remembering Lori

Somewhere concealed behind an ivied fence, pressed between stiff suburban walls, a tiny patch of garden grows, fruitful as a bit of Eden, tended by what seems like, enchantresses, but most likely is any familiar gardener. Somehow, though there are many undiscovered secrets, Earth is persuaded to procreate by these gardeners who then become one with that which they tend, that which they stoked to bloom. Lush abundance of the soil is at last released. When the sun descends, with fatigue put aside, gardeners share an undisturbed respite to study the rich abundance, the quiet dazzle of plants. Narrowing light blends flowers, shrubs and trees en masse making a Monetesque sanctuary where now the rows of roses nod their unbiased heads in the breezes of the dusk.

Judith Cody is a poet, composer and photographer who has won national awards in these fields. Her poems are published in over 160 journals. A poem won second place in the national Soul-Making Keats Literary Competition; a poem is in the Smithsonian's Institution's permanent collection in Spanish and English editions; poems were quarter-finalists for the Pablo Neruda Prize and won honorable mentions from the National League of American Pen Women. Cody was Editor-in-Chief of the first "Resource Guide on Women in Music," from San Francisco State University; she edited the PEN Oakland anthology, "Fightin' Words." Books include the internationally noted biography of the American composer, "Vivian Fine: A Bio-Bibliography," also "Eight Frames Eight, poems" and the poem "Woman Magic". A poem was chosen from a world competition by Centre College's Norton Center for the Arts to be featured in a year-long exhibit highlighting artistic relationships between literature and photography. Judith's photo essay of a rare World War Two B-17 aircraft ranks number one on Google out of 220 million. She received the University of California Master Gardener lifetime achievement award.

Say hello at: www.judithcody.com

www.ingramcontent.com/pod-product-compliance
Lightning Source LLC
LaVergne TN
LVHW041512070426
835507LV00012B/1502